Contents

Introduction ....
Guide to Purchasing a Stroller ....
Walk 1: Hyde Park Circular......................
Walk 2: Central London & St James Park
Walk 3: Regent's Park & Primrose Hill ....
Walk 4: Bridges of Central London.. 10
Walk 5: Battersea Park & Power Station 13
Walk 6: Greenwich Park Circuit... 14
Walk 7: Scadbury Park & Petts Wood 17
Walk 8: Shepherdleas & Oxleas Woods... 19
Walk 9: Nonsuch Park Circular.. 21
Walk 10: Richmond Park & Hill 23
Walk 11: Kingston to Hampton Court Palace.................................... 24
Walk 12: Virginia Water Lake 27
Walk 13: Windsor Great Park – Long Walk...................................... 29
Walk 14: Ruislip Lido Circular.. 31
Walk 15: Little Venice & Grand Union Canal 33
Walk 16: Highbury to Finsbury: Capital Ring 34
Walk 17: Hampstead & Parliament Hill... 37
Walk 18: Camden Lock & Regent's Canal 39
Walk 19: Queen Elizabeth Olympic Park.. 41
Walk 20: Epping Forest Circular 43

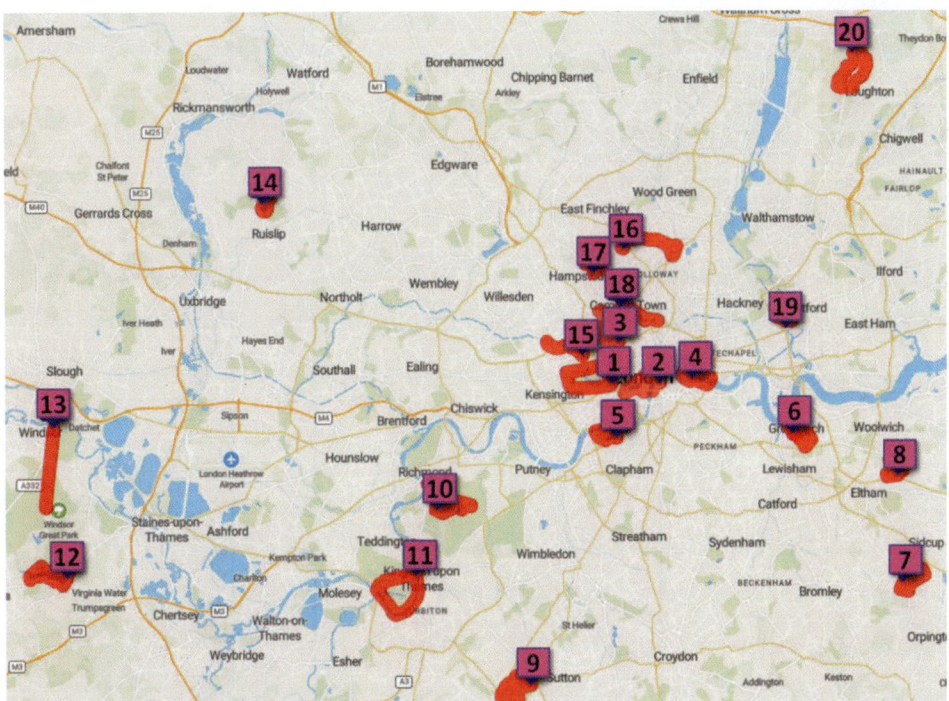

1

Introduction

London is one of the great cities in the world to explore by foot. There is a huge variety of architecture, spectacular views and natural urban spaces to enjoy. This guide presents twenty varied family walks in and around London that can be explored with a buggy.

Map Legend

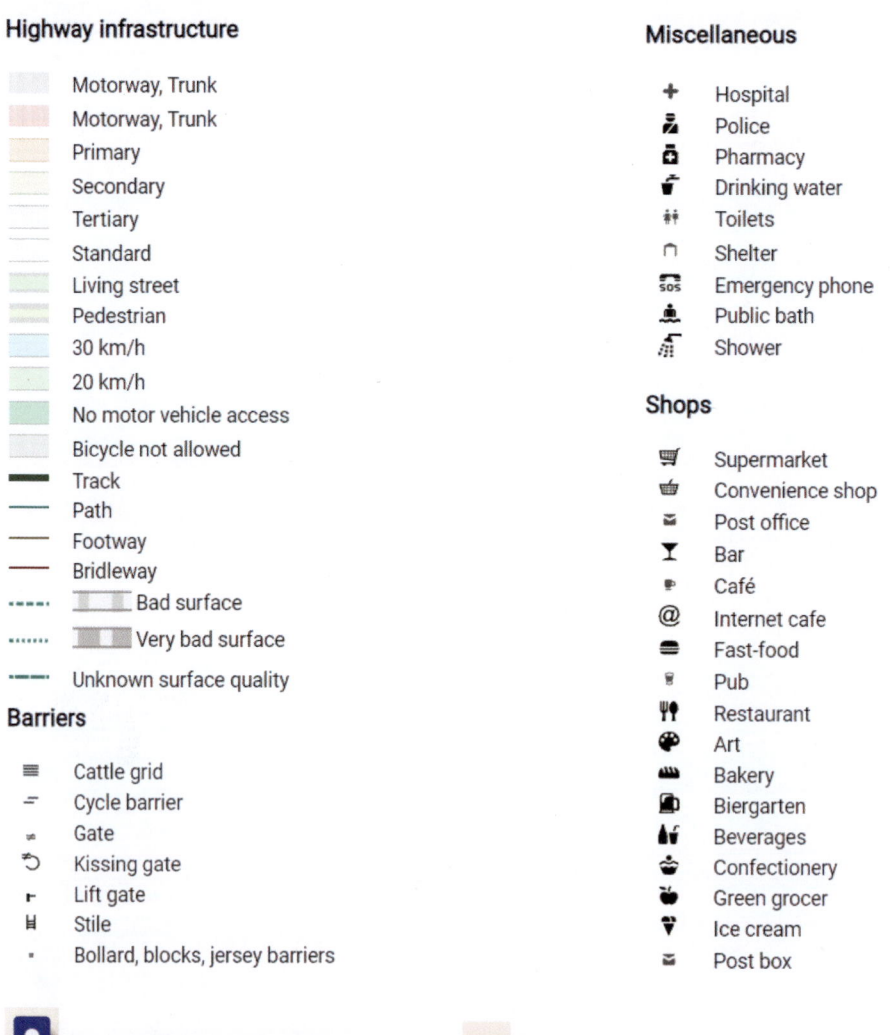

Highway infrastructure

- Motorway, Trunk
- Motorway, Trunk
- Primary
- Secondary
- Tertiary
- Standard
- Living street
- Pedestrian
- 30 km/h
- 20 km/h
- No motor vehicle access
- Bicycle not allowed
- Track
- Path
- Footway
- Bridleway
- Bad surface
- Very bad surface
- Unknown surface quality

Barriers

- Cattle grid
- Cycle barrier
- Gate
- Kissing gate
- Lift gate
- Stile
- Bollard, blocks, jersey barriers

Miscellaneous

- Hospital
- Police
- Pharmacy
- Drinking water
- Toilets
- Shelter
- Emergency phone
- Public bath
- Shower

Shops

- Supermarket
- Convenience shop
- Post office
- Bar
- Café
- Internet cafe
- Fast-food
- Pub
- Restaurant
- Art
- Bakery
- Biergarten
- Beverages
- Confectionery
- Green grocer
- Ice cream
- Post box

Start/End of Walk   Route

2

Guide to Walking Buggies

A wide variety of buggies and strollers are available, with different features and designs. For regular walking use, a hiking stroller designed for outdoor use over terrain is recommended.

Hiking buggies often have suspension and larger wheels with thicker and more durable tyres than a traditional stroller, enabling them to handle rougher terrain. Hiking strollers are often larger and heavier than regular strollers, making them more robust and better suited for carrying infants and toddlers on long hikes or walks. Wheels at least 12in in size with pneumatic tyres are recommended for rough terrain, with good clearance around the wheels to avoid clogging with mud and leaves.

Traditional strollers are most suited for use on walks on paved and prepared pathways.

All walks in this guide are subjectively graded for flatness and smoothness of surface (a higher star rating = a relatively smoother and flatter route).

Walk 1: Hyde Park Circular

Distance:	4.2 miles
Surface Smoothness:	★★★★☆
Flatness:	★★★★☆
Nearest Station:	Hyde Park Corner Underground
Nearest Parking:	Park Lane, W1K 1AB
Start Point:	Queen Elizabeth Gate, W1J 7NT
Look out for:	Kensington Palace & Speaker's Corner.

Hyde Park is the largest of the four Royal Parks in Central London, and has many points of interest through the seasons. This route follows the outer perimeter of the park, with several points of interest on the way including Kensington Palace, Queen Victoria statue and The Serpentine. A generally flat walk with a few small inclines, mostly on gravel and paved paths.

Walk 2: Central London & St James Park

Distance:	4.5 miles
Surface Smoothness:	★★★★★
Flatness:	★★★★★
Nearest Station:	London Waterloo Train Station
Nearest Parking:	Cornwall Rd, SE1 9PP
Start Point:	1 Charlie Chaplin Walk, SE1 8XR
Look out for:	Buckingham Palace, St James Place, Trafalgar Square, Houses of Parliament, Downing Street & The London Eye

An iconic walk through the heart of London, visiting several key attractions, including Downing Street and Buckingham Palace. The route passes through St James Park and along a varied stretch of the River Thames in Westminster. A flat walk on gravel and paved paths.

Walk 3: Regent's Park & Primrose Hill

Distance:	4.5 miles
Surface Smoothness:	★★★☆☆
Flatness:	★☆☆☆☆
Nearest Station:	Great Portland St Underground
Nearest Parking:	Bank Park, W1W 5AU
Start Point:	Park Square, NW1 4LH
Look out for:	Queen Mary's Rose Gardens & Panoramic Views London from Primrose Hill

A walk with spectacular views over Central London. The walk starts in Regent's Park, before climbing Primrose Hill and then winding back through the park. The walk finishes with a visit to Queen Mary's Rose Gardens and the Japanese Garden Island. A hilly walk mostly on gravel or paved paths, but with some unprepared sections.

Walk 4: Bridges of Central London

Distance:	3.0 miles
Surface Smoothness:	★★★★★
Flatness:	★★★★★
Nearest Station:	London Bridge Train Station
Nearest Parking:	Kipling St, SE1 3RU
Start Point:	Park Square, NW1 4LH
Look out for:	HMS Belfast, Tower of London, Tower Bridge and Tate Modern

This interesting walk follows the River Thames through Central London, crossing the famous Tower Bridge and Millennium Bridge. This flat walk also passes a number of key London landmarks, including the Tower of London and HMS Belfast. The walk is on paved paths.

Walk 5: Battersea Park & Power Station

Distance:	2.8 miles
Surface Smoothness:	★★★★☆
Flatness:	★★★★★
Nearest Station:	Battersea Park Train Station
Nearest Parking:	Queenstown Road, SW11 8PP
Start Point:	Park Lane, SM3 8BU
Look out for:	London Peace Pagoda & Battersea Power Station

Battersea Park is a 200-acre green space situated on the south bank of the River Thames opposite Chelsea. This varied walk encompasses riverside stretches, lakes, monuments and open parkland. The walk is largely flat and on a mix of paved and graded surfaces.

Walk 6: Greenwich Park Circuit

Distance: 2.8 miles
Surface Smoothness: ★★★★★
Flatness: ★★★☆☆
Nearest Station: Greenwich Train Station
Nearest Parking: Burney St, SE10 8EX
Start Point: St Mary's Gate, SE10 9JL
Look out for: Royal Observatory Greenwich, Cutty Sark & Maritime Museum

This walk through Greenwich Park overlooks the River Thames and has some of London's most iconic views. Greenwich Park is an amazing mix of 17th century landscape, stunning gardens and a rich history that dates back to Roman times. Paved paths with some moderate climbs.

15

Walk 7: Scadbury Park & Petts Wood

Distance: 3.0 miles
Surface Smoothness: ★★☆☆☆
Flatness: ★★★☆☆
Nearest Station: Chiselhurst Train Station (1.5mi)
Nearest Parking: Old Perry Street, BR7 6PT
Start Point: The Drive, BR7 6QE
Look out for: Scadbury Manor

Scadbury Park is a Local Nature Reserve in Chislehurst in the London Borough of Bromley, and is part of an extensive wildlife corridor along with Petts Wood. This walk explores the woodland and the historic Scadbury Manor. Unsealed paths with potential for mud after rain. Some gentle climbs.

Walk 8: Shepherdleas & Oxleas Woods

Distance:	3.1 miles
Surface Smoothness:	★☆☆☆☆
Flatness:	★★☆☆☆
Nearest Station:	Falconwood Train Station
Nearest Parking:	Crown Woods Ln, SE18 3JA
Start Point:	Rochester Way, SE9 2RD
Look out for:	Bluebells (~April-May)

Oxleas Wood is one of the few remaining areas of ancient deciduous forest in southeast London, with some parts dating back over 8,000 years. This walk explores the woodlands, and is particularly beautiful in Springtime. Unsealed paths which will be muddy after rain, with some moderate climbs.

Walk 9: Nonsuch Park Circular

Distance:	3.1 miles
Surface Smoothness:	★★★☆☆
Flatness:	★★☆☆☆
Nearest Station:	Cheam Train Station
Nearest Parking:	The Avenue, SM3 8DP
Start Point:	Park Lane, SM3 8BU
Look out for:	Nonsuch Mansion

Nonsuch Park is a large partially-wooded Park with a range of wildlife and a rich history. Nonsuch Mansion is located in the centre of the park. This peaceful walk is on a mix of paved and grass paths, and can get muddy after extensive rain. The park has some moderate hills.

Walk 10: Richmond Park & Hill

Distance:	4.8 miles
Surface Smoothness:	★★★☆☆
Flatness:	★★★☆☆
Nearest Station:	Richmond Train Station
Nearest Parking:	Queens Road, TW10 5HX
Start Point:	Park Lane, SM3 8BU
Look out for:	Richmond Hill, King Henry's Mound, Sawyer Hill Views, Pen Ponds & The Royal Ballet School

This walk explores a beautiful and green area of London, with wide views to the West and also into the City. The walk is on a mixture of grass and gravel paths, past lakes and through woodland. A few moderate inclines.

Walk 11: Kingston to Hampton Court Palace

Distance:	4.2 miles
Surface Smoothness:	★★★★☆
Flatness:	★★★★★
Nearest Station:	Kingston Train Station
Nearest Parking:	Old Bridge Street, KT1 4DP
Start Point:	Old Bridge Street, KT1 4DP
Look out for:	Hampton Court Palace

A peaceful walk along the River Thames from Kingston-upon-Thames to Hampton Court Palace, the previous residence of King Henry VIII. The walk returns through Bushy Park, the second largest of London's Royal Parks. A flat walk mostly on gravel paths.

Walk 12: Virginia Water Lake

Distance: 4.5 miles
Surface Smoothness: ★★★★★
Flatness: ★★★★☆
Nearest Station: Virginia Water Train Station
Nearest Parking: London Rd, GU25 4QF
Start Point: London Rd, GU25 4QF
Look out for: Leptis Magna Roman Ruins,
                       Totem Pole & Cascade Waterfall

This walk follows the woodland shores of this magnificent lake. This area is steeped in a rich history that spans centuries – from ancient monuments to cascading waterfalls and stunning vistas. A flat walk mostly on gravel paths.

Walk 13: Windsor Great Park – Long Walk

Distance:	5.9 miles (there and back)
Surface Smoothness:	★★★★★
Flatness:	★★★★☆
Nearest Station:	Windsor & Eton Train Station
Nearest Parking:	Victoria St, SL4 1EG
Start Point:	Park St, SL4 1LU
Look out for:	Windsor Castle & Deer Herds

The Long Walk is an historic 3 mile avenue from Windsor Castle to the Copper Horse Statue. This tree-lined avenue stretches from the ancient fortress deep into the Windsor Great Park. A straightforward walk on a paved path with a shallow slope towards one end.

Walk 14: Ruislip Lido Circular

Distance: 1.6 miles
Surface Smoothness: ★★★★☆
Flatness: ★★★★☆
Nearest Station: Ruislip Underground Station
Nearest Parking: Reservoir Road, HA4 7TY
Start Point: Reservoir Road, HA4 7TY
Look out for: Ruislip Lido Railway, Ruislip Lido Beach & Woodland Centre

Ruislip Lido is a 60-acre lake with sandy beaches, a miniature railway, multiple play areas and peaceful woodland walks. This walk circuits the perimeter of the Lido on gravel and paved paths. There are multiple options to extend the walk into the woodland.

Walk 15: Little Venice & Grand Union Canal

Distance: 3.2 miles (there and back)
Surface Smoothness: ★★★★★
Flatness: ★★★★★
Nearest Station: Paddington Train Station
Nearest Parking: Bishop's Bridge Road, W2 6AA
Start Point: Paddington Green, W2 1LG
Look out for: Little Venice

This walk follows an interesting stretch of the Grand Union Canal from Paddington to Meanwhile Gardens. The route passes through Little Venice which is a picturesque canalside area. A flat and straightforward walk on paved paths.

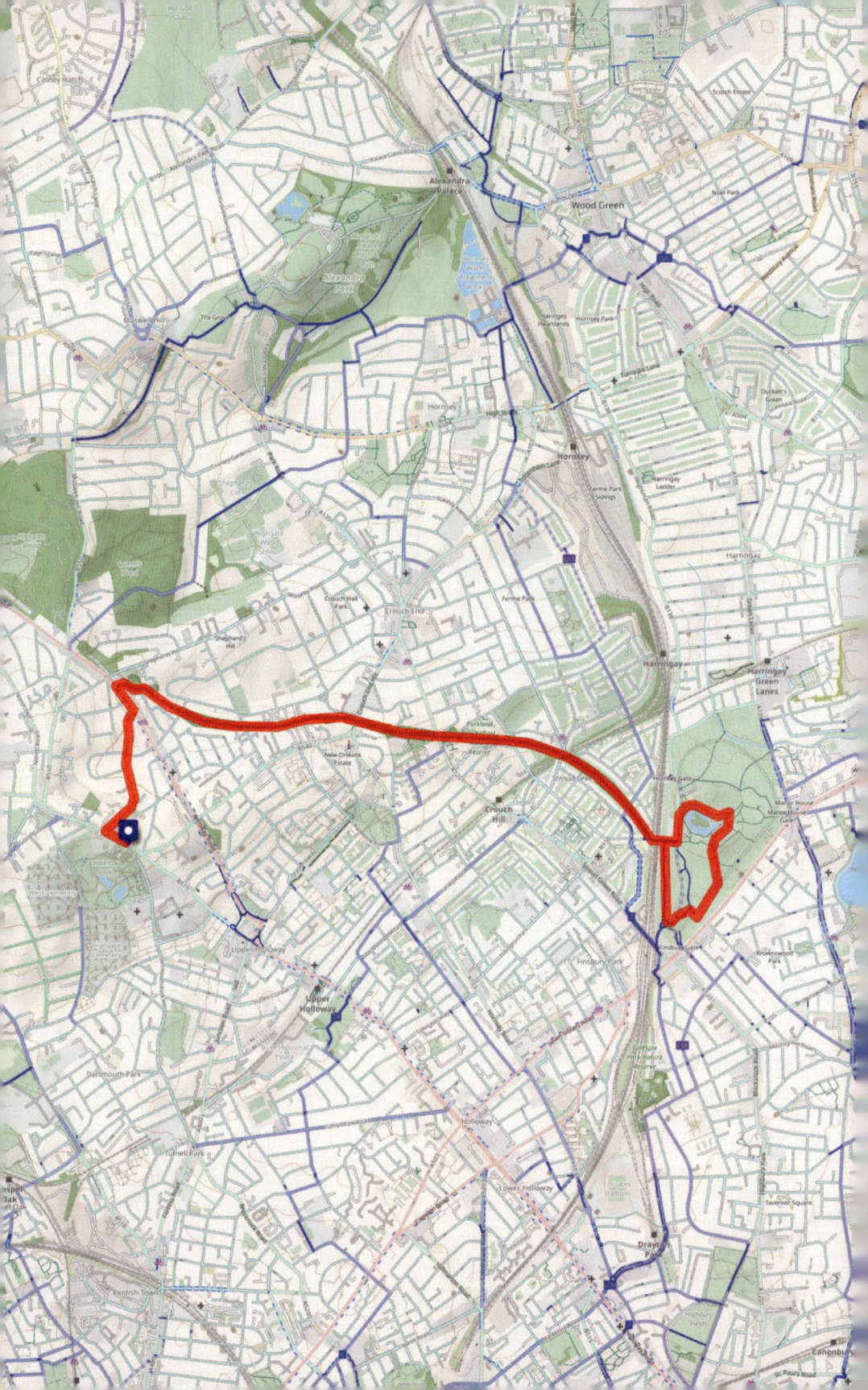

Walk 16: Highbury to Finsbury: Capital Ring

Distance: 5.9 miles (there and back)
Surface Smoothness: ★★★★☆
Flatness: ★★★★☆
Nearest Station: Archway Underground Station
Nearest Parking: Highgate Hill, N19 5NQ
Start Point: Highgate Hill, London N6 5HG
Look out for: Highbury Cemetery & Finsbury Park

An urban route from Highbury to Finsbury Park. Finsbury Park was one of the first of the great London parks laid out in the Victorian era. A flat and straightforward walk on a mixture of gravel and paved paths.

Walk 17: Hampstead & Parliament Hill

Distance:	2.2 miles
Surface Smoothness:	★★☆☆☆
Flatness:	★☆☆☆☆
Nearest Station:	Hampstead Heath Station
Nearest Parking:	E Heath Rd, London NW3 1TH
Start Point:	E Heath Rd, London NW3 1TH
Look out for:	Parliament Hill Viewpoint & Viaduct Bridge

Hampstead Heath is a wild park with woodlands and meadows, with spectacular views of the city from Parliament Hill. This short loop walk captures some highlights from the park. The hilly path is on a variety of prepared and unprepared surfaces.

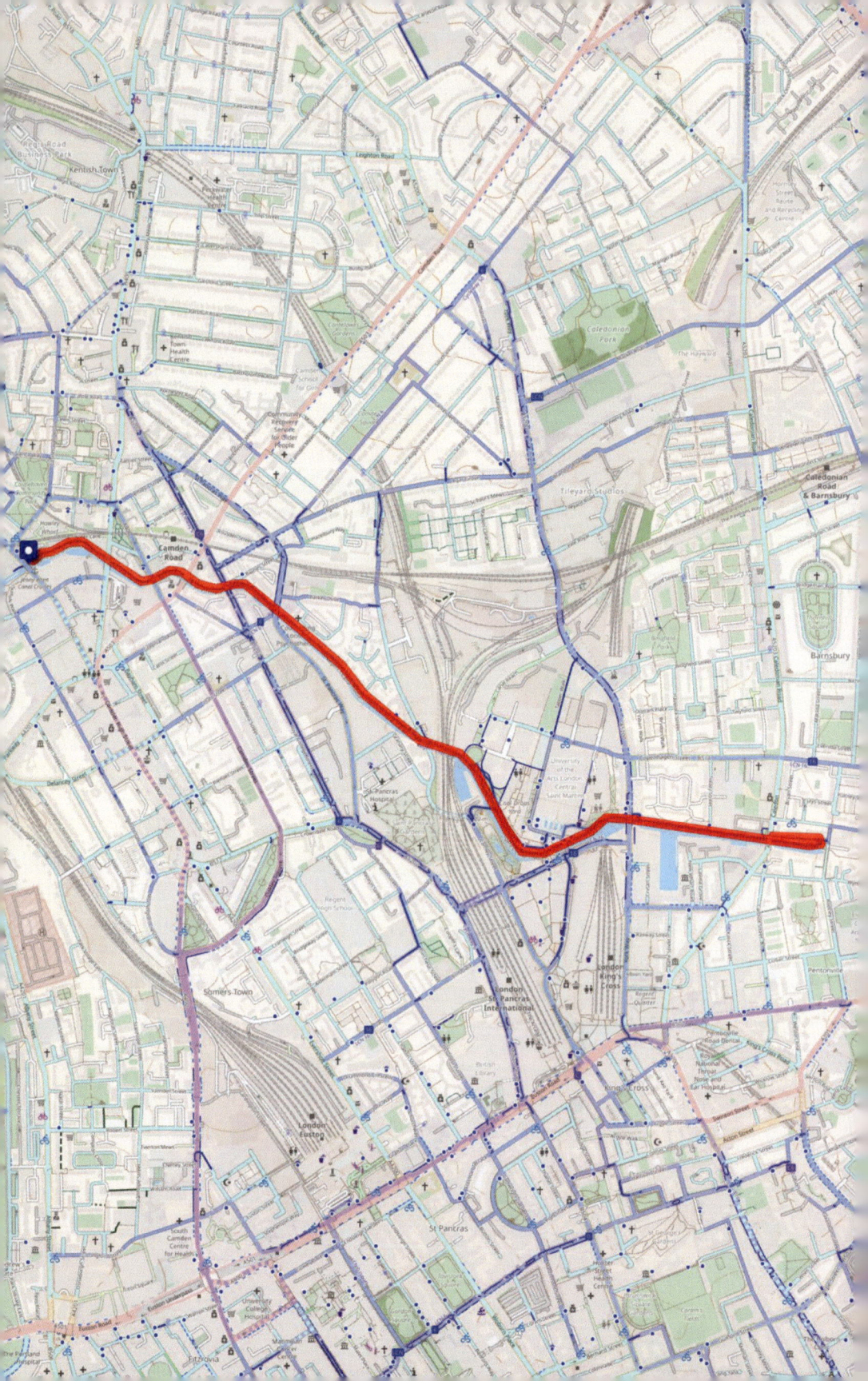

Walk 18: Camden Lock & Regent's Canal

Distance: 2.2 miles (there and back)
Surface Smoothness: ★★★★★
Flatness: ★★★★★
Nearest Station: Camden Town Undergrnd Station
Nearest Parking: 38-40 Pratt St., London NW1 0LY
Start Point: Middle Yard, London NW1 8AL
Look out for: Camden Lock, Gasholder Park & Granary Square

This walk follows an interesting stretch of the famous Regent's Canal from Camden Town through to Kings Cross. A flat and straightforward walk on paved paths along the Regent's Canal with varied architecture and scenery.

Walk 19: Queen Elizabeth Olympic Park

Distance:	3.0 miles
Surface Smoothness:	★★★★☆
Flatness:	★★★★☆
Nearest Station:	Pudding Mill Lane DLR Station
Nearest Parking:	2 St Marks Gate, London E9 5HT
Start Point:	Barbers Rd, London E15 2PJ
Look out for:	ArcelorMittal Orbit & Great British Garden

Queen Elizabeth Olympic Park is a sporting complex and public park in east London. It was purpose-built for the 2012 Summer Olympics and Paralympics. This walk covers a number of points of interest on a mixture of paved and graded flat paths.

41

Walk 20: Epping Forest Circular

Distance:	5.5 miles
Surface Smoothness:	★☆☆☆☆
Flatness:	★★☆☆☆
Nearest Station:	Loughton Underground Station
Nearest Parking:	Rushey Pln, Loughton IG10 4AE
Start Point:	Highgate Hill, London N6 5HG
Look out for:	Epping Forest Visitors Centre

Epping Forest is a 2,400-hectare area of ancient woodland which is a former royal forest. This circuit explores one of the main trails in the forest, with many opportunities to see varied wildlife. A walk with some inclines on unprepared forest tracks. There is a potential for the paths to become muddy after rain.

Enjoy your Adventures with family in London

© 2022

Further Information & Walking Safely: *Every effort has been made to present information as accurately as possible, but 100% accuracy cannot be guaranteed. Anyone choosing to use content in this book and participate in their own independent activities does so entirely at their own risk. It cannot be guaranteed that all paths will remain in the same condition should they be affected by factors including potentially adverse weather, obstructions, diversion's and any other situations affecting the condition of the land. The authors cannot be held responsible for your interpretation of the walks and other information provided. You are responsible for your own safety when walking. It is essential that you are properly equipped and clothed for walking and that you have the appropriate map. Car parks and public transport referenced in the guide are chargeable, and may be liable to change.*